PEGASUS ENCYCLOPEDIA LIBRARY

Space
EARTH

Edited by: Pallabi B. Tomar, Hitesh Iplani
Managing editor: Tapasi De
Designed by: Vijesh Chahal, Anil Kumar, Rohit Kumar
Illustrated by: Suman S. Roy, Tanoy Choudhury
Colouring done by: Vinay Kumar, Kiran Kumari & Pradeep Kumar

CONTENTS

Introduction 3

Formation of the Earth 4

Evolution of life on Earth 6

Earth as a planet 8

Earth's size and shape 9

Composition and structure 11

Tectonic plates 14

Rotation and Orbit 15

Influence of the sun and the moon 17

Spheres of the Earth 19

Gravity of the Earth 23

Rocks of the Earth 24

Cycles on and within the Earth 27

Earth in culture 30

Test Your Memory 31

Index 32

Introduction

Earth is a small planet in the vastness of space. It is one of nine planets that travel through space around the sun. The sun is a star, one of the billions of stars that make up a galaxy called the Milky Way. The Milky Way along with many as 100 billion other galaxies make up the universe.

The planet Earth is only a tiny part of the universe, but it is the home of human beings and in fact, all known life in the universe. Animals, plants and other organisms live almost everywhere on the Earth's surface. They can live on Earth because it is just the right distance from the sun. Most living things need the sun's warmth and light for life. If the Earth had been too close to the sun, it would have been too hot for living things. If the Earth had been too far from the sun, it would have been too cold for anything to survive. Living things also must have water to live. Earth has plenty. Water covers most of the Earth's surface.

> The study of Earth is called geology and the scientists who study Earth are geologists.

Formation of the Earth

The Earth was formed approximately 4.6 billion years ago. The exact details of the formation of Earth are not known, but scientists have been able to develop a theory describing the events. Radioisotopic dating has aided scientists in forming theories that depict the formation of Earth.

It is beleived that the Earth was formed along with our solar system from a large cloud of spinning gas and dust. The spinning cloud of gas and dust eventually began to shrink due to gravity. As this happened, it slowly formed into a flatted disk rotating around a central core, which eventually became our sun. Over time, particles that were present in the dust cloud began to stick together and eventually formed planetesimals. A planetesimal is an object formed from dust, rock and other materials. Planetesimals can be anywhere in size from several metres to hundreds of kilometres. The term refers to small celestial bodies formed during the creation of planets. Larger planetesimals were able to attract smaller planetesimals due to their gravitational pull. Over time, planetesimals collided with one another due to gravity, which resulted in the formation of the planets in our solar system.

Astonishing fact

From a distance, Earth would be the brightest of the 9 planets. This is because sunlight is reflected on the planet's water!

Formation of the Earth

Geodesy is the branch of applied mathematics concerned with measuring or determining the shape of the Earth, its gravitational field and the location of fixed points.

In the very beginning of Earth's history, this planet was a giant, red hot, boiling sea of molten rock—a magma ocean. The heat had been generated by the repeated high speed collisions of much smaller bodies of space rocks that continually clumped together as they collided to form this planet. As the collisions tapered off, the Earth began to cool, forming a thin crust on its surface. As the cooling continued, water vapour began to escape and condense in the Earth's early atmosphere. Clouds formed and storms raged, raining more and more water down on the primitive Earth, cooling the surface further until it was flooded with water, forming the seas.

It is theorized that the true age of the Earth is about 4.6 billion years, formed at about the same time as the rest of our solar system. The oldest rocks geologists have been able to find are 3.9 billion years old!

5

Evolution of life on Earth

After the formation of the planet Earth, it could not support life, for about a quarter of age. About billion years ago, our planet condensed to form a swirling cloud of interstellar dust and gas. The surface was too hot to allow the existence of protoplasm (the stuff of living cells). Even

> One-tenth of the Earth's surface is always under ice. And almost 90 per cent of that ice is to be found in the continent of Antarctica.

water, a major component of protoplasm was present only as vapour, one among many other gases in the hot, murky atmosphere.

About 3.5 million years ago life first began in water. Life arose from the non-living organic matter dissolved or suspended in water. All living objects originated from non-living material. The development of photosynthesis allowed the sun's energy to be harvested directly by life forms. The resultant oxygen accumulated in the atmosphere and formed a layer of ozone (a form of molecular oxygen [O3]) in the upper atmosphere. The incorporation of smaller cells within larger ones resulted in the development of complex cells called **eukaryotes**. True multicellular organisms formed as cells within colonies became increasingly specialized. Aided by the absorption of harmful ultraviolet radiation by the ozone layer, life was established on the surface of the Earth.

Evolution of life on Earth

Scientists have studied rocks using radiometric dating methods to determine the age of Earth. Another really helpful thing they have found in rocks which tell us more about the story of Earth's past are the remains of living creatures that have been embedded in the rocks since many ages. We call these fossils. It has been the careful study of Earth's fossil record that has revealed the exciting picture about the kinds of creatures that once roamed this planet. Fossilized skeletons of enormous creatures with huge claws and teeth, ancient ancestors of modern day species (such as sharks) that have remained virtually unchanged for millions of years and prehistoric jungles lush with plant life, all point to a abundance of life and a variety of species that continues to populate the Earth, even in the face of periodic mass extinctions.

Fossil of archaeopteryx

Human being constituted the pinnacle of evolution of life forms. Human beings have been on Earth for some 2 million years which is less than 1/1000 of the time for which life existed on Earth. Human beings are highly evolved species endowed with intelligence far superior to that of any other organism.

Astonishing fact

Worldwide, each day, 400 billion gallons (1,514,164,712,000 litres) of water is used!

EARTH

Earth as a planet

Earth ranks fifth in size among the nine planets. It has a diameter of about 13,000 km. Jupiter, the largest planet, is about 11 times larger in diameter than Earth. Pluto, (now called the 'dwarf planet') has a diameter less than one-fifth that of the Earth.

Earth, like all the planets in our solar system, travels around the sun in a path called an **orbit**. Earth is about 150 million km away from the sun. It takes one year for the Earth to complete one orbit around the sun. The innermost planet, Mercury, is only about one-third as far from the sun as the Earth and circles the sun in only 88 days. Pluto, is 40 times as far from the sun as the Earth and takes 248 Earth years to circle the sun!

Astonishing fact

Approximately 70 per cent of the Earth's surface is covered by water, but unfortunately 97 per cent of this water is saline which is present in the various oceans of the world and hence of no use.

Earth's size and shape

Earth's size

As the largest of the terrestrial planets, Earth has an estimated mass of 5.9736 × 1024 kg. Its volume is also the largest of the planets at 108.321 × 1010km³.

In addition, Earth is the densest of the terrestrial planets as it is made up of a crust, mantle and core. The Earth's crust is the thinnest of these layers while the mantle comprises 84 per cent of Earth's volume and extends 2,900 km below the surface. What makes Earth the densest of these planets however is its core. Earth's average density is 5515 × 10 kg/m³. Mars, the smallest of the terrestrial planets by density, is only around 70 per cent as dense as the Earth.

Earth is classified as the largest of the terrestrial planets based on its circumference and diameter as well. At the equator, Earth's circumference is 40,075.16 km. It is slightly less between the North and South poles at 40,008 km. Earth's diameter at the poles is 12,713.5 km while it is 12,756.1 km at the equator. For comparison, the largest planet in Earth's solar system, Jupiter has a diameter of 142,984 km.

> The distance from the surface of Earth to its centre is about 6,378 km.

EARTH

Earth's shape

Earth's circumference and diameter differ because its shape is classified as an oblate spheroid or ellipsoid, instead of a sphere. This means that instead of being of equal circumference in all areas, the poles are squished, resulting in a bulge at the equator, and thus a larger circumference and diameter there.

The equatorial bulge at the Earth's equator is measured at 42.72 km and is caused by the planet's rotation and gravity. Gravity itself causes planets and other celestial bodies to contract and form a sphere. This is because it pulls all the mass of an object as close to the centre of gravity (the Earth's core in this case) as possible.

As the Earth rotates, this sphere is distorted by the centrifugal force. This is the force that causes objects to move outward away from the centre of gravity. Therefore, as the Earth rotates, centrifugal force is greatest at the equator so it causes a slight outward bulge there, giving that region a larger circumference and diameter.

Astonishing fact

The lowest point on the Earth's surface exists in the Dead Sea in the Middle East which is about 400 m below sea level.

Composition and structure

Earth's interior structure includes the crust, mantle, inner core and outer core. The crust and mantle are rocky. The inner and outer cores are metallic.

People often think of the planet Earth as being mostly made by water because most of Earth's surface is covered by water. However, the interior composition and structure of the Earth is quite different from its surface. Earth's interior is mostly rocky or metallic and is layered into the crust, mantle, inner core and outer core with the denser metallic materials concentrated towards the centre.

Earth's crust

The crust is the Earth's outermost layer, and it is the only layer that scientists can directly study. Earth's crust ranges from 8 to 70 km thick. It is solid and has a rocky composition. The top portion of the crust is the only portion of Earth's interior that geologists can study directly.

The crust is divided into tectonic plates that float on the mantle. The slow drifting of these tectonic plates causes most of the Earth's geological processes.

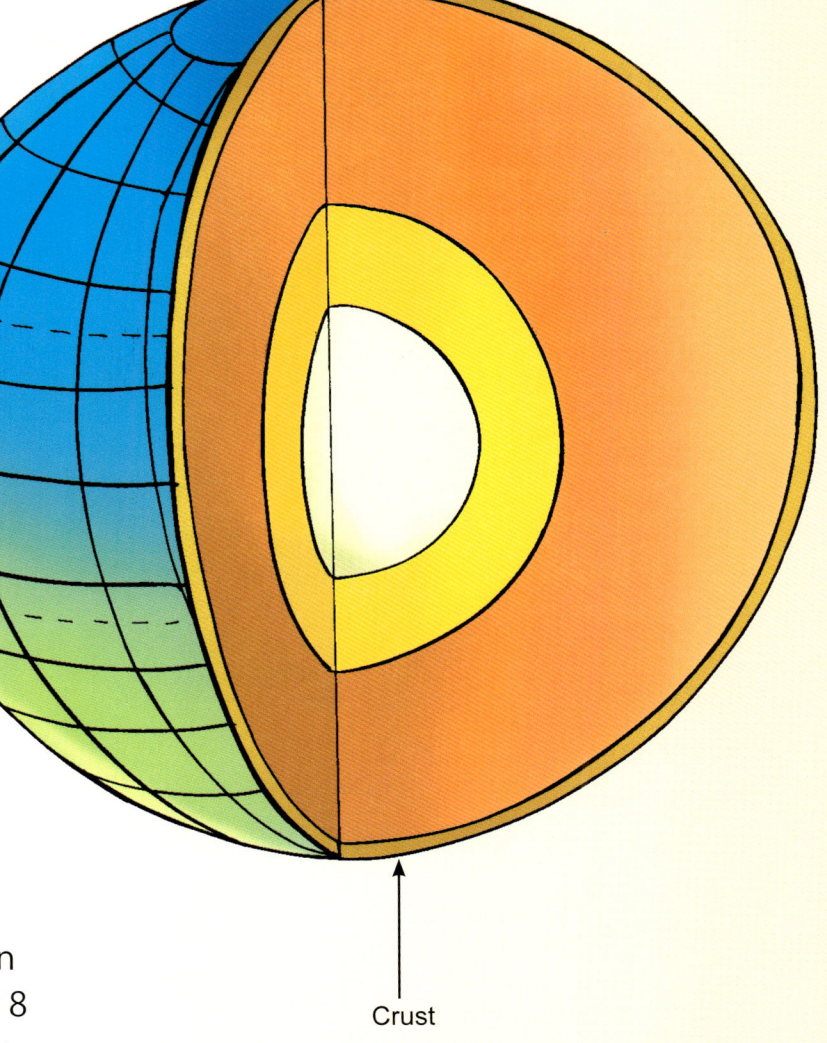
Crust

Astonishing fact

The temperature of Earth near the centre is thought to be at least 3,870 degree Celsius!

EARTH

Earth's mantle

Like the crust, Earth's mantle has a rocky composition. Most people would describe the rocky mantle as being solid, however technically it is not really solid. The mantle is in a semi-solid state that can flow very slowly.

Heat sources in the core cause convection currents in the slowly flowing mantle. These convection currents cause the continental plates in Earth's crust to drift and transfer heat energy from Earth's core to the upper mantle and crust.

Earth's mantle is about 2900 km thick.

Astonishing fact

Other planets and moons in our solar system have volcanoes, but they do not have mountain ranges like the Earth because only Earth has plate tectonics.

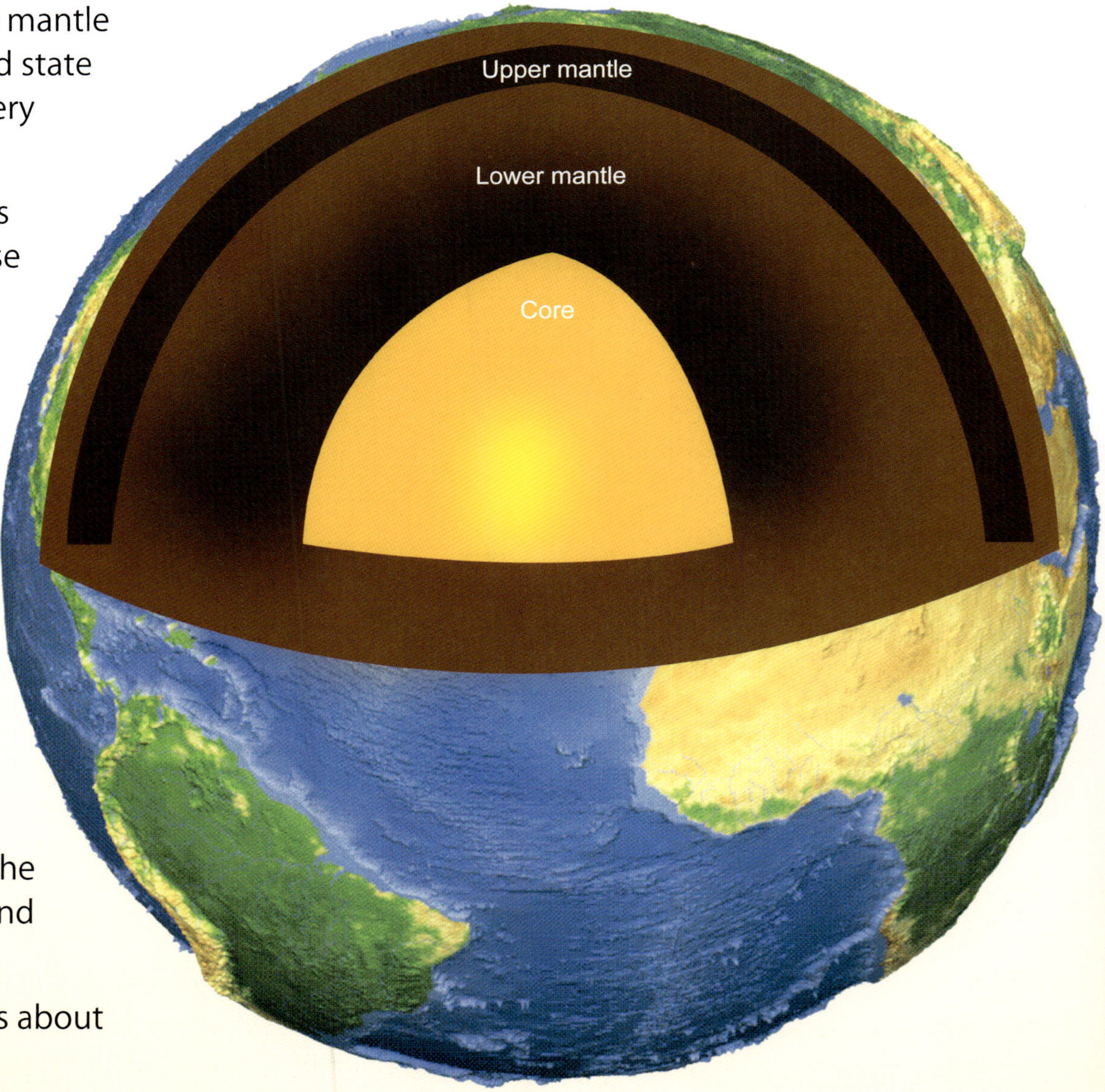

Composition and structure

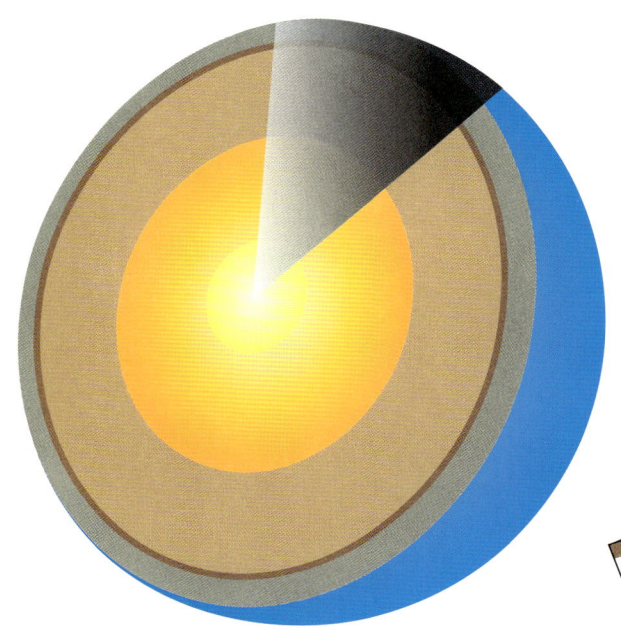

Astonishing fact

Most of the Earth's deserts are not composed entirely of sand. About 85 per cent of them are rocks and gravel.

Earth's core

The inner part of the Earth is the **core**. This part of the Earth is about 2,900 km below the Earth's surface. The core is a dense ball of the elements iron and nickel. It is divided into two layers, the inner core and the outer core. The inner core or the centre of the Earth is solid and about 1,250 km thick. The outer core is so hot that the metal is always molten, but the inner core pressures are so great that it cannot melt, even though

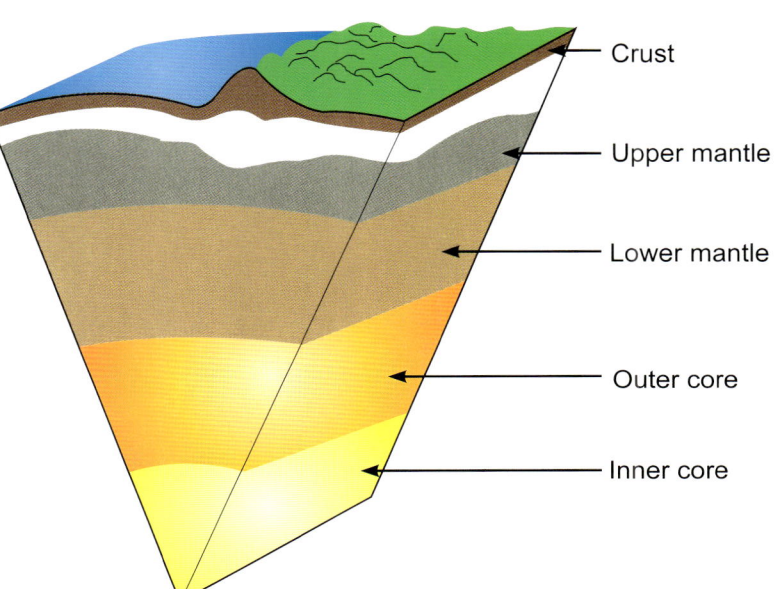

temperatures there reach 3700 degrees Celsius. The outer core is about 2,200 km thick. As the Earth rotates, the outer core spins around the inner core and that causes the Earth's magnetism.

Astonishing fact

Pangaea or the undivided landmass was not the beginning position of the land on Earth, but one of the six lost worlds that have come and gone. Pangaea was preceded by Pannotia about 550-650 million years ago and by Rhodinia around 1.8 billion years ago. Before them, at intervals of roughly 500 million years, Nuna, Kenorland, and Ur existed and then broke up.

Tectonic plates

Tectonic plates are large plates of rock that make up the foundation of the Earth's crust and the shape of the continents. The tectonic plates comprise the bottom of the crust and the top of the Earth's mantle. There are ten major plates on the Earth and many more minor ones. They float on a plastic-like part of the Earth's mantle called the **asthenosphere**. The plates are most famously known for being the source of earthquakes. When plates push up against each other, they create mountain ranges and volcanoes. Mt. Everest was created in this manner.

With time, plate tectonics has caused the world's continents to be reshaped. Every continent on Earth was once a part of an ancient supercontinent known as Pangaea, and Antarctica was once located in a temperate climate. Marine fossils can be found on the peaks of the world's tallest mountains. The tectonic plates continue to move slowly, but it is unlikely that their movement will cause the world's face to change more rapidly than the growing technological influence of mankind.

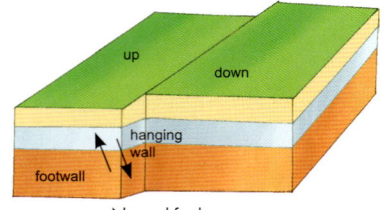
Normal fault

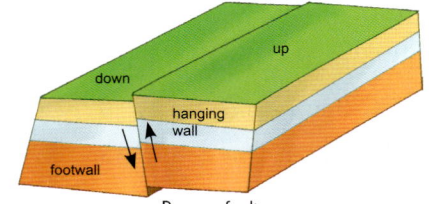
Reverse fault

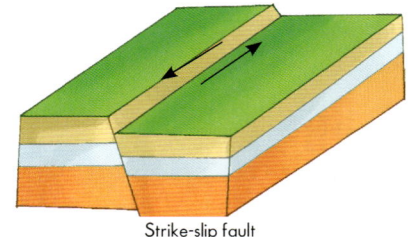
Strike-slip fault

Astonishing fact

Plate tectonics contributed to making Earth habitable by creating volcanoes. The water vapour and other gases emitted by volcanoes during Earth's early years helped to create Earth's oceans and atmosphere.

Rotation and Orbit

The Earth's rotation

The term Earth's rotation refers to the spinning of our planet on its axis. If the Earth is viewed from the North Pole from space, you will notice that the direction of rotation is counter-clockwise. The opposite is true if the Earth is viewed from the South Pole. One rotation takes twenty-four hours and is called a **mean solar day**.

The Earth is constantly rotating around an axis (called its rotational axis). Some objects rotate about a horizontal axis, like a rolling log. Some objects, such as a skater, rotate about a vertical axis. The Earth's axis is tipped over about 23.5 degree from vertical.

The Earth rotates around once in 24 hours—a rate of 1609 km per hour! The time it takes for the Earth to rotate completely around once is what we call a day. The Earth's rotation is responsible for the daily cycles of day and night. At any one moment in time, one half of the Earth is in sunlight, while the other half is in darkness. The Earth's rotation also creates the apparent movement of the sun across the horizon.

The combined effect of the Earth's tilt and its motion on its orbital path results in seasons.

> The amount of carbon dioxide in water and atmosphere and the amount of solar energy the planet receives are two factors that control the future of life on Earth and the planet itself.

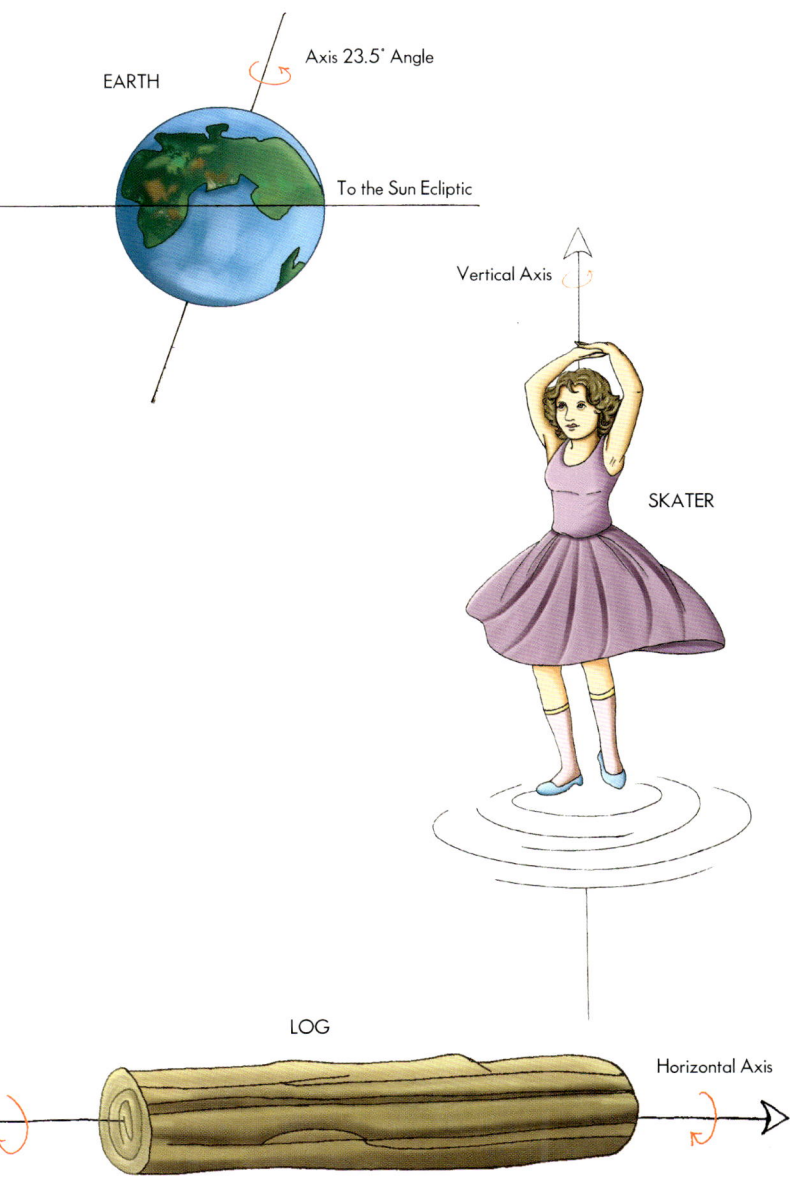

EARTH

Orbit of Earth

The Earth's orbit is the motion of the Earth around the sun at an average distance of about 150 million km. Earth's travels around the sun on an elliptical orbit. This means there are times when the Earth is closer and times that it's further from the sun.

The closest point of this elliptical orbit is called the **perihelion**. At this point, the Earth is only 147 million km from the sun. At its furthest point, which astronomers call **aphelion**, Earth is 152 million km.

There's a significant difference between these two points. And this can actually vary the amount of sunlight that reaches our planet. The perihelion happens in January when the northern hemisphere is tilted away from the sun experiencing winter. The southern hemisphere is tilted towards the sun experiencing summer. Earth takes 365.256 days to complete one orbit around the sun.

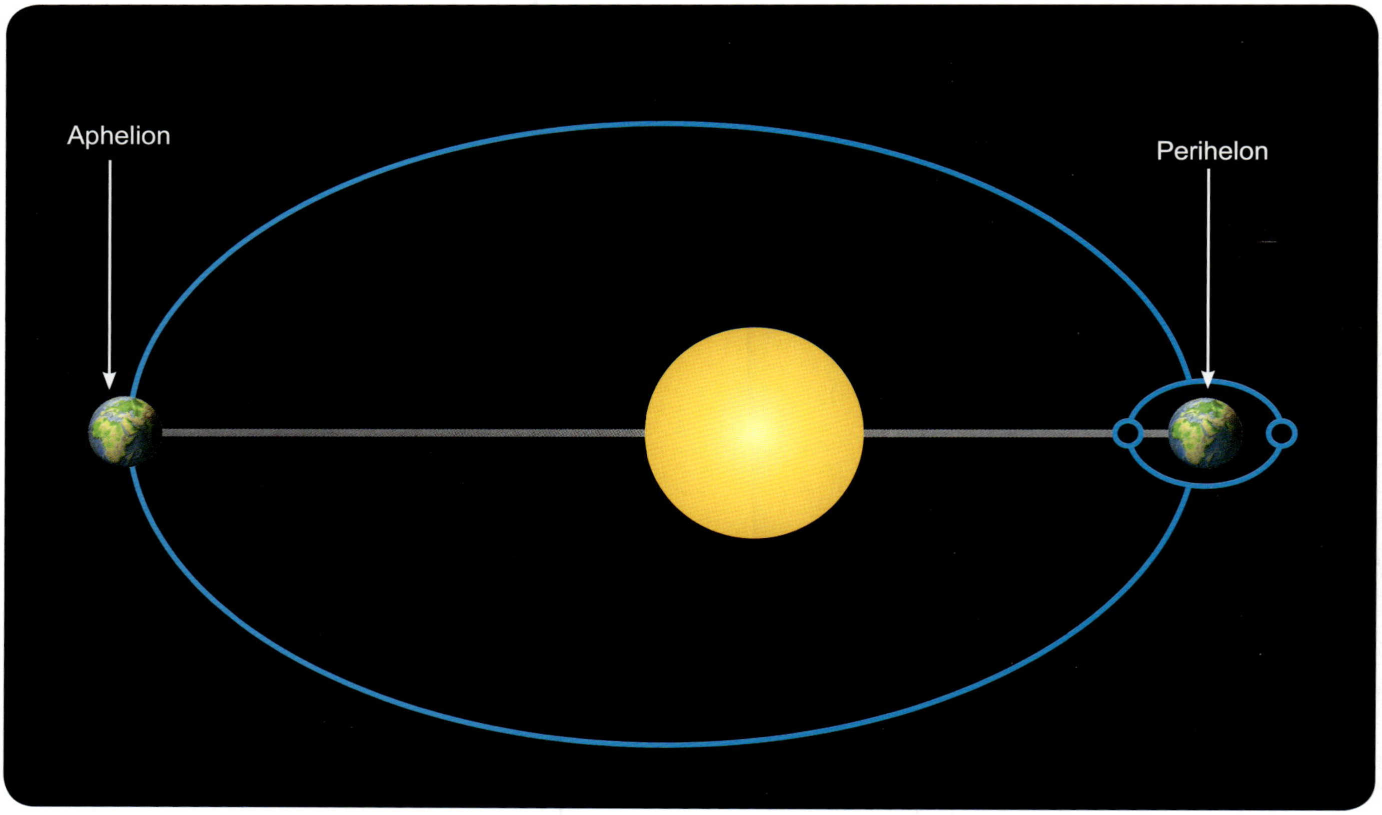

Aphelion — Perihelon

Astonishing fact

Earth, which can be viewed as a metal ball coated with rock, hurtles through space at 107,000 km per hour!

Influence of the sun and the moon

The moon orbits the Earth and in turn, the Earth orbits the sun. We see the universe from a platform that is both rotating on its axis, and travelling in an elliptical orbit around the sun. The Earth's rotation on its axis makes the sun rise in the east and set in the west. It is also a big part of why the moon rises and sets too; although, the moon takes 29 days to complete an orbit around the Earth as well.

The average distance from the Earth to the moon is 384,403 km and the average distance from the Earth to the sun is 149,597,887 km. If you divide these two numbers, you get approximately 389. Now, if you divide the diameter of the sun (1.4 million km) by the diameter of the moon (3,474 km), you get 403. Those two numbers are pretty close. This is why the moon and the sun appears to be the same size in the sky.

Astonishing fact

The birth of Earth's moon is extremely important because it stabilizes the Earth's tilt. Without the moon, Earth would have wild changes in the climate and be uninhabitable. The stabilizing tug of the moon tempers Earth, resulting in the minor tip that causes seasons.

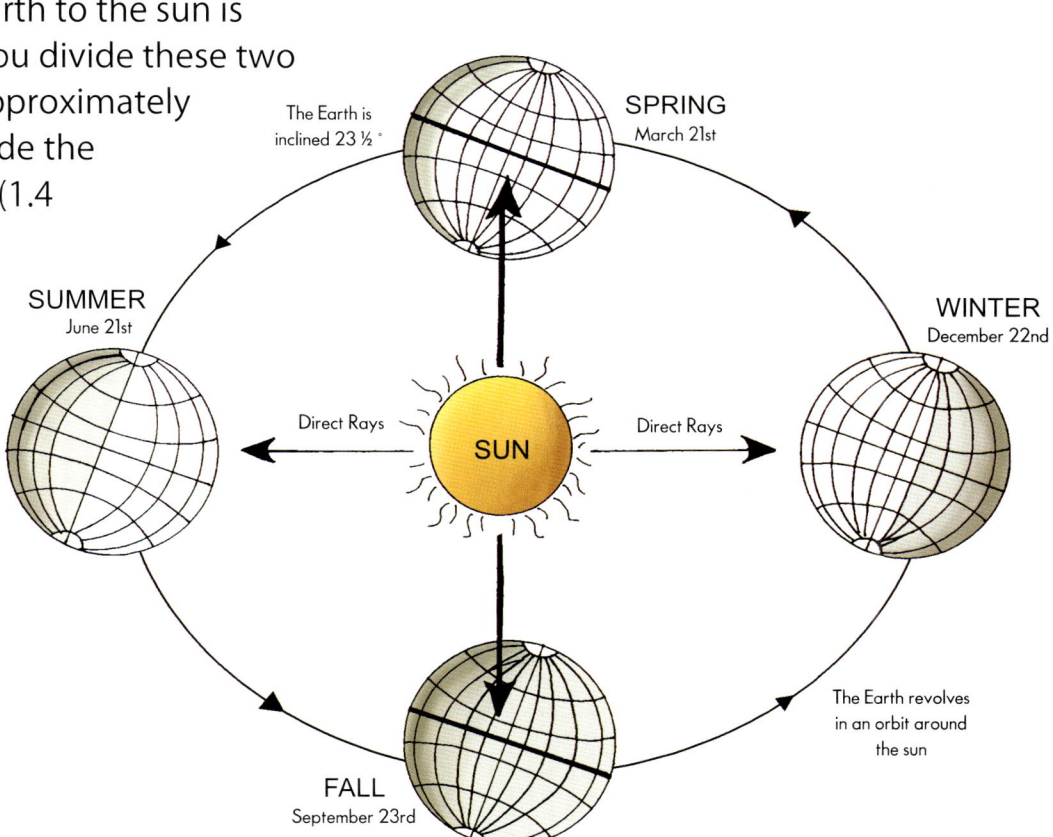

EARTH

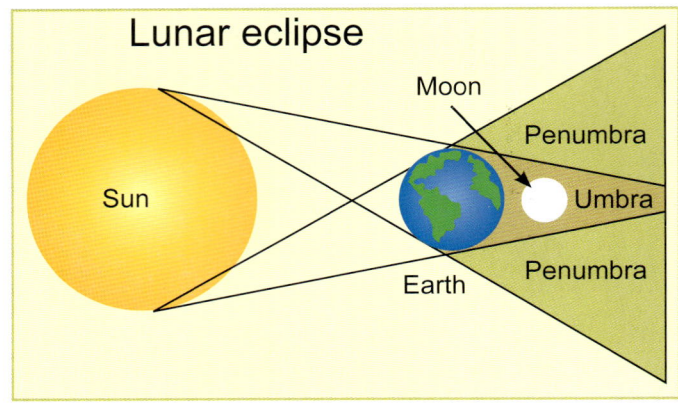

As they appear to be the same size in the sky, the sun, Earth and the moon work together to create eclipses. When the moon is directly in between the Earth and sun, we see a solar eclipse. The moon appears to pass in front of the sun and darken it completely. And in the opposite situation, when the Earth is in between the sun and the moon, the Earth's shadow darkens the moon. This is a lunar eclipse. We don't see eclipses every month because the moon's orbit is tilted slightly away from the Earth's orbit around the sun. Sometimes the moon is above this orbit and sometimes it's below, so it doesn't block the light from the sun, or get caught in the Earth's shadow.

The sun and the moon work together to create the tides we experience here on Earth. Most of the rise in the tides comes from the gravitational pull of the moon, but a small amount comes from the sun.

Lunar eclipse

When the two heavenly bodies are on the same side of the Earth, we get the highest and the lowest tides, and when they are on opposite sides of the Earth, the tides are less extreme.

The brightest object in the sky is the sun and all of the moon's brightness is just the reflected light from the sun.

Astonishing fact

One of the driest places on the planet, Antarctica receives precipitation in the form of rain or snowfall only about once or twice a year.

Spheres of the Earth

Earth is composed of several layers, or spheres, somewhat like the layers of an onion. The solid Earth consists of a thin outer layer, the crust, with a thick rocky layer, the mantle, beneath it. The crust and the upper portion of the mantle are called the **lithosphere**. At the centre of the Earth is the core. The outer part of the core is liquid, while the inner part is solid. Much of the Earth is covered by a layer of water or ice called the **hydrosphere**. Earth is surrounded by a thin layer of air, the **atmosphere**. The portion of the hydrosphere, atmosphere, and solid land where life exists is called the **biosphere**.

Atmosphere

The atmosphere contains all the air in the Earth's system. It extends from less than 1 m below the planet's surface to more than 10,000 km above the planet's surface. The upper portion of the atmosphere protects the organisms of the biosphere from the sun's ultraviolet radiation. It also traps heat. When air temperatures in the lower portion of this sphere changes, weather occurs. As air in the lower atmosphere is heated or cooled, it moves around the planet. The result can be as simple as a breeze or as complex as a tornado.

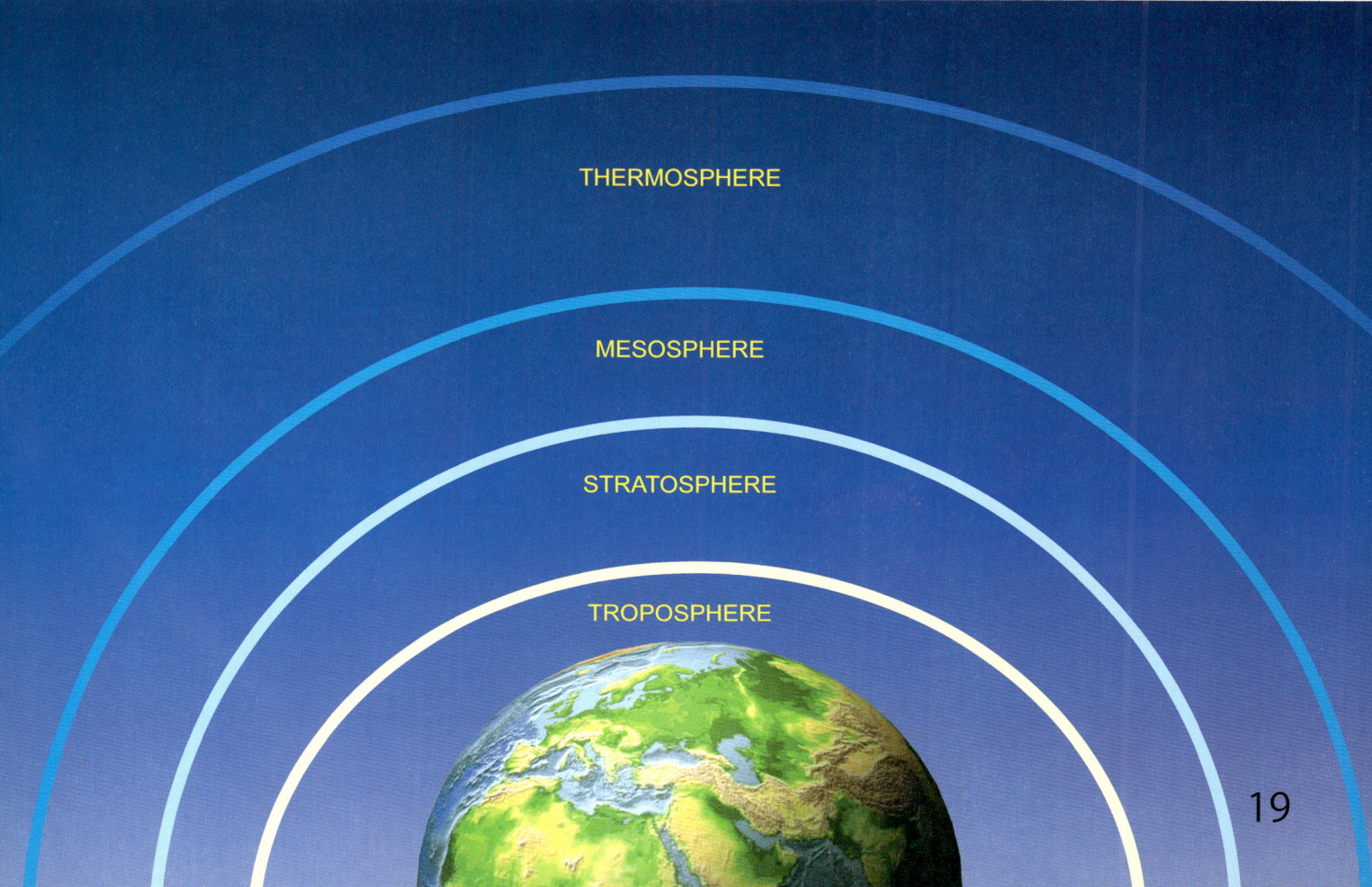

EARTH

Astonishing fact

Although Earth's plates are made of solid rock, they buckle and twist like slabs of warm clay when they collide.

Hydrosphere

Earth is the only planet in the solar system with abundant liquid water on its surface. Water has chemical and physical properties not matched by any other substance, and it is essential for life on Earth. Water has a great ability to absorb heat. The oceans store much of the heat Earth gets from the sun. The electrical charges on water molecules give water a great ability to attract atoms from the other substances. This quality allows water to dissolve many things. Water's ability to dissolve materials makes it a powerful agent in breaking down rocks. Liquid water on Earth affects not just the surface but the interior as well. Water in the rocks lowers the melting temperature of rocks. Water dramatically weakens rocks and makes them easier to melt beneath Earth's surface.

About 71 per cent of Earth's surface is covered by water, most of it in the oceans. Ocean water is too salty to drink. Only about 3 per cent of Earth's water is fresh water, suitable for drinking. Much of Earth's fresh water is not readily available to people because it is frozen in the polar ice caps or beneath Earth's surface. Polar regions and high mountains stay cold enough for water to remain permanently frozen. The region of permanent ice on Earth is sometimes called the **cryosphere**.

Lithosphere

The lithosphere contains all of the cold, hard solid land of the planet's crust (surface), the semi-solid land underneath the crust, and the liquid land near the centre of the planet. The surface of the lithosphere is very uneven. There are high mountain ranges like the Rockies and Andes, huge plains or flat areas like those in Texas, Iowa, and Brazil and deep valleys along the ocean floor.

The solid, semi-solid, and liquid land of the lithosphere form layers that are physically and chemically different. If someone were to cut the Earth through its centre, these layers would be revealed like the layers of an onion. The outermost layer of the lithosphere consists of loose soil rich in nutrients, oxygen and silicon. Beneath that layer lies a very thin, solid crust of oxygen and silicon. Next is a thick, semi-solid mantle of oxygen, silicon, iron, and magnesium. Below that is a liquid outer core of nickel and iron. At the centre of Earth is a solid inner core of nickel and iron.

Astonishing fact

The sun's diameter is about 109 times greater than Earth's, whereas the Earth is just about four times larger in diameter than the moon.

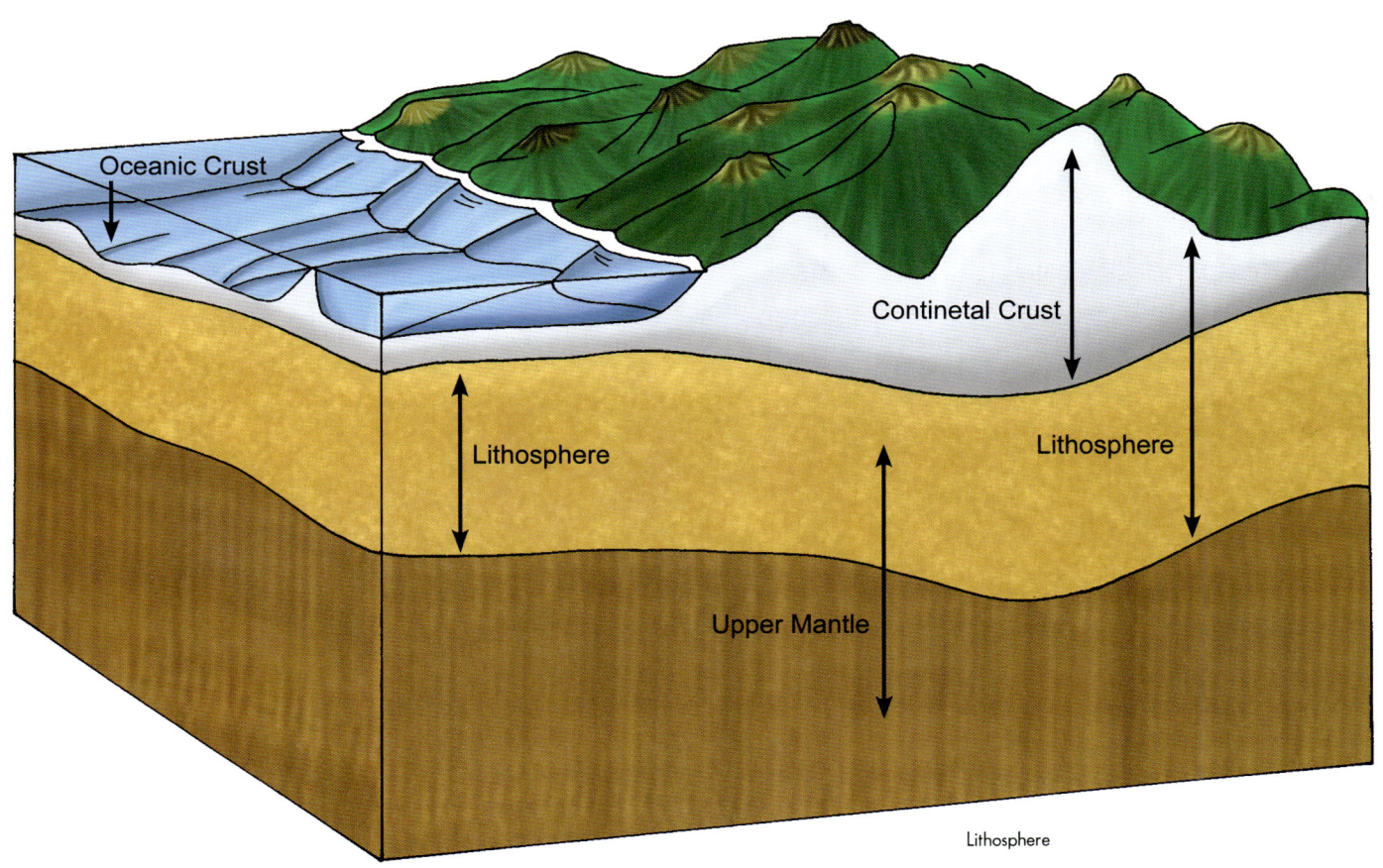

EARTH

Biosphere

The biosphere contains all the planet's living things. This sphere includes all of the microorganisms, plants and animals of Earth.

Within the biosphere, living things form ecological communities based on the physical surroundings of an area. These communities are referred to as biomes. Deserts, grasslands and tropical rainforests are three of the many types of biomes that exist within the biosphere.

Life affects Earth in many ways. Life has actually made the atmosphere around us. Plants take in water and carbon dioxide, both of which contain oxygen. They use the carbon in carbon dioxide and the hydrogen in water to make chemicals of many kinds and give off oxygen as a waste product. Animals eat plants to get energy and return water and carbon dioxide back into the environment.

Living things affect the surface of Earth in other ways as well. Plants create chemicals that speed the breakdown of rocks. Grasslands and forests slow the erosion of soil.

Astonishing fact

If you could evaporate all the water out of all the oceans and spread the resulting salt over all the land on Earth, you would have a 152 m layer coating everything.

Gravity of the Earth

Gravity causes the Earth to move around the sun. This phenomenon not only causes the Earth to keep moving around the sun, but also to keep the moon rotating around the Earth and it makes things fall to the ground. All matter, even the smallest object, has a gravitational force. The heavier the object, the stronger is its gravitational force.

The sun is far away but it's very heavy and has a big gravitational force with respect to the Earth. Due to the great speed, the Earth has the tendency to fly away from the sun. The gravity of the sun stops this, so that the Earth stays in its orbit. This also happens when you swing around an object on a rope. You feel the power by which you keep the item in its orbit as long as you keep swinging the rope. When you let it go, the item shoots outwards.

The Earth is also a big and heavy 'object' and also has a big gravity. This is why we keep staying on the ground and that everything you let go, falls to the ground. The moon spins around the Earth and keeps moving by the attraction of the Earth in the same way as the Earth keeps moving around the sun. But the moon also has its attraction to the Earth. We can see this every day on the beach when we witness the movements of high tide and low tide.

Astonishing fact

The 2.5 km thick ice sheet covering the continent of Antarctica constitutes around 90 per cent of the total fresh water. It is the largest store of fresh water on the planet.

Rocks of the Earth

The solid part of Earth consists of rocks, which are sometimes made up of a single mineral, but more often consist of mixtures of minerals. Geologists classify rocks according to their origin. Igneous rocks form when molten rock cools and solidifies. Sedimentary rocks form when grains of rock or dissolved chemicals are deposited in layers by wind, water or glaciers. Over time, the layers harden into solid rock. Metamorphic rocks develop deep in the Earth's crust when heat or pressure transforms other types of rock.

Igneous rocks

Igneous rocks form from molten material called **magma**. Most of Earth's interior is solid, not molten, but it is extremely hot. At the base of Earth's crust, the temperature is about 1000 degrees Celsius. In some portions of the crust, conditions are right for rocks to melt. Rocks can melt more easily near the crust if they contain water which lowers their melting point.

> **Rocks are like the Earth's blood because Earth's levels of air and water are kept in balance by the continuous circulation of rocks.**

Astonishing fact

More than 80 per cent of the Earth's surface is made up of volcanic matter.

Sedimentary rocks

Sedimentary rocks make up about three-quarters of the rocks on the Earth's surface. They form at the surface in environments such as beaches, rivers, oceans and anywhere where sand, mud and other types of sediment collect. Sedimentary rocks preserve a record of the environments that existed when they formed. By looking at sedimentary rocks of different ages, scientists can figure out how climate and environments have changed through Earth's history. Fossils of ancient living things are preserved in sedimentary rocks too.

Many sedimentary rocks are made from the broken bits of other rocks. These are called **clastic** sedimentary rocks. The broken bits of rocks are called sediment. Sediment is the sand you find on the beach, the mud in a lake bottom, the pebbles in a river, and even the dust on furniture. The sediment may, in time, form a rock if the little pieces become cemented together.

There are other types of sedimentary rocks whose particles do not come from broken rock fragments. Chemical sedimentary rocks are made of mineral crystals such as halite and gypsum formed by chemical processes. The sediment particles of organic sedimentary rocks are the remains of living things such as clamshells, plankton skeletons, dinosaur bones and plants.

EARTH

Metamorphic rocks

When rocks are buried deeply, they become hot. Earth's crust grows hotter by about 25 degrees Celsius per km of depth. Pressure also increases with depth. As rocks are heated and subjected to pressure, minerals react and the rocks become metamorphic. Shale is transformed to slate, limestone eventually into marble under pressure.

Some rocks only change a little, while others change a lot. When a rock is metamorphosed, its mineral crystals change. Usually, the same chemical ingredients are used to form new crystals during metamorphism. Sometimes new types of minerals grow that weren't in the rock before.

The temperatures on the Earth range from -88 degree to 58 degree Celsius. 100 million years ago it was 6 to 12 degrees hotter than it is today. Alligators lived in what is now ice-covered Greenland.

Cycles on and within the Earth

Earth can be thought of as a huge system of interacting cycles. The cycles affect everything on the planet, from the weather to the shape of the landscape. There are many cycles on and within the Earth. A few of the most important are:

1. Atmospheric circulation
2. Ocean currents
3. The global heat conveyor
4. Hydrologic cycle
5. Rock cycle

Atmospheric circulation

The atmosphere, a thin blanket of gases that surrounds Earth, transports heat and water and filters out deadly ultraviolet radiation. Whether it is just a gentle breeze or a hurricane-force gale, Earth's atmosphere is constantly on the move.

When the atmosphere moves, it evens out differences in temperature between the chilly poles and the warm equator. Warm air from the equator moves toward the poles and cold air from the poles moves toward the equator. This circulation of air is disrupted a bit by the Earth's rotation. This makes counterclockwise winds around hurricanes, winter storms, tornadoes, and other low-pressure areas north of the equator and clockwise south of the equator.

Astonishing fact

The Pacific Ocean is one of the largest features on the face of the Earth, with an area of more than 181 million square km. It contains half of the world's water!

Ocean currents

Ocean currents are driven by the winds and follow the same general pattern. The continents block the flow of water around the globe, so ocean currents flow west near the equator, then turn toward the poles when they strike a continent, turn east, then flow back to the equator on the other side. In all the oceans, the ocean currents form great loops called **gyres**. The gyres flow clockwise north of the equator and counter clockwise south of it.

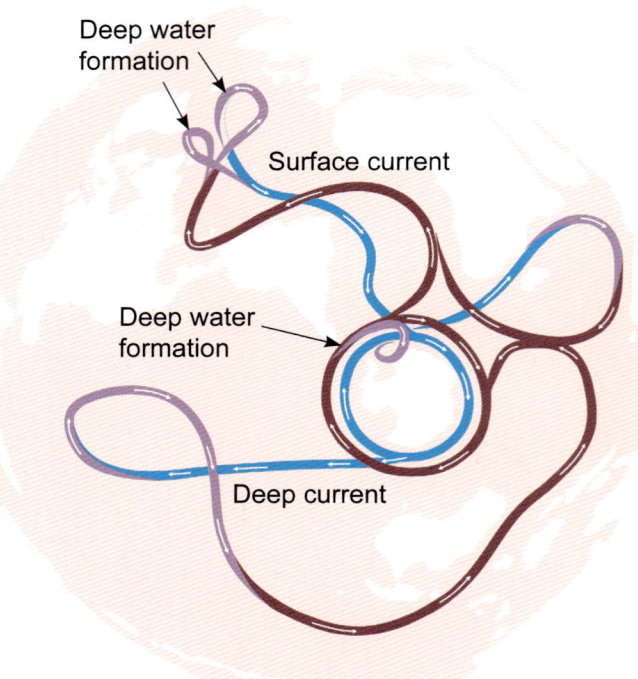

The global heat conveyor

The global heat conveyor

The global heat conveyor is an enormous cycle of ocean water that distributes the oceans heat around Earth. Water in the Polar regions is very cold, salty and dense. It sinks and flows along the sea floor toward the equator. Eventually, the water rises along the margins of the continents and merges with the surface water flow. When it reaches the Polar regions, it sinks again. This three-dimensional movement of water mixes heat throughout the oceans, warming polar waters. It also brings nutrients up from the deep ocean to the surface, where they are available for marine plants and animals.

> It takes light 8 minutes 20 seconds to travel from the sun to the Earth.

Cycles on and within the Earth

Hydrologic cycle

Water from the oceans evaporates and is carried by the atmosphere, eventually falling as rain or snow. Water that falls on the land helps break rocks down chemically, nourishes plants, and wears down the landscape. Eventually, the water returns to the sea to start the cycle over again.

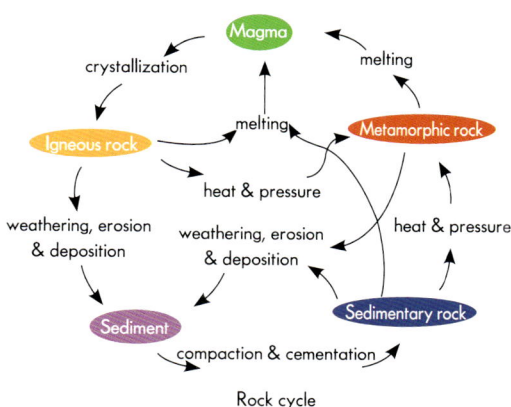

Rock cycle

Rock cycle

Earth has many kinds of rocks compared to other planets because there are so many processes acting to form and break down rocks. Geologists sometimes speak of the rock cycle to explain how different rock types are related. The cycle may begin with a flow of lava from a volcano cooling to form new igneous rocks on Earth's surface. As the rock is exposed to water, it breaks down and the resulting materials maybe carried away to be deposited as sedimentary rocks. These rocks may eventually be so deeply buried that they change in form to become metamorphic rocks. They may even melt, creating the raw material for the next generation of igneous rocks.

Astonishing fact

Earth doesn't take 24 hours to rotate on its axis. It's actually 23 hours, 56 minutes and 4 seconds.

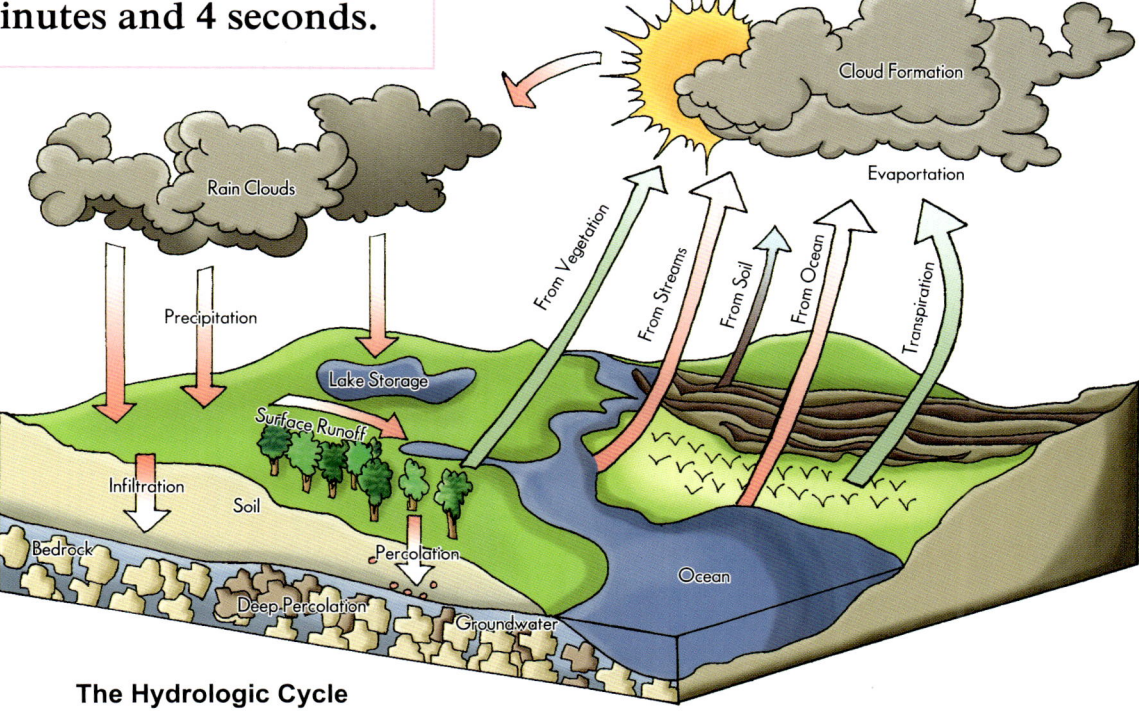

The Hydrologic Cycle

29

Earth in culture

The name 'Earth' derives from the Anglo-Saxon word 'erda', which means 'ground or soil'. It is the only name for a planet of the solar system that does not come from Greco-Roman mythology. The standard astronomical symbol of the Earth consists of a cross circumscribed by a circle.

Unlike the rest of the planets in the Solar System, mankind did not recognize the Earth as a planet until the 16th century. Earth has often been personified as a deity, in particular a goddess. Creation myths in many religions recall a story involving the creation of the Earth by a supernatural deity or deities.

In the past there were varying levels of belief in a flat Earth, but this was displaced by the concept of a spherical Earth due to observation and circumnavigation. The human perspective regarding the Earth has changed following the advent of spaceflight and the biosphere is now widely viewed from a globally integrated perspective. This is reflected in a growing environmental movement that is concerned about mankind's effects on the planet.

Astonishing fact

A belief of some Native Americans was that the Earth is supported by a giant tortoise, which made the Earth tremble each time it took a step.

Test Your MEMORY

1. What is the Earth?

2. Write briefly about how the Earth was formed.

3. How did life evolve on Earth?

4. Write about the size and shape of the Earth?

5. What is the Earth composed of?

6. Write briefly about the orbit and rotation of the Earth?

7. Write what you know about the sun and the moon?

8. Describe briefly the spheres of the Earth.

9. Write about the gravitational force of Earth.

10. Write briefly about the Earth's rocks.

11. Write about the cycles on and in Earth.

12. How did the name Earth come into being?

Index

A
aphelion 16
asthenosphere 14
atmosphere 5, 6, 14, 15, 19, 22, 27, 29
atmospheric circulation 27

B
biosphere 19, 22, 30

C
celestial bodies 4, 10
centrifugal force 10
clastic 25
continents 14, 28
core 4, 9, 10, 11, 12, 13, 19, 21
crust 5, 9, 11, 12, 14, 19, 21, 24, 26
cryosphere 20

D
dating 4, 7

E
ellipsoid 10
elliptical orbit 16, 17
equator 9, 10, 27, 28
eukaryotes 6

G
galaxy 3
geologists 3, 5, 11, 24, 29

gravity 4, 10, 23
gyres 28

H
human being 7
hydrologic cycle 27, 29
hydrosphere 19

I
Igneous rocks 24
inner core 11, 13, 21
interstellar 6

J
Jupiter 8, 9

L
lithosphere 19, 21
lunar eclipse 18

M
magnetism 13
mantle 9, 11, 12, 14, 19, 21
Mercury 8
Metamorphic rocks 24, 26
Milky Way 3
Mt. Everest 14

N
northern hemisphere 16

O
oblate spheroid 10
ocean currents 27, 28

orbit 8, 16, 17, 18, 23
outer core 11, 13, 21

P
perihelion 16
planet 3, 6, 7, 8, 9, 10, 11, 15, 16, 18, 19, 20, 21, 22, 23, 27, 30
planetesimals 4
Pluto 8
protoplasm 6

R
radiation 6, 19, 27
rock cycle 27, 29

S
Sedimentary rocks 24, 25
solar eclipse 18
southern hemisphere 16
sphere 10, 19, 22
sun 3, 4, 6, 8, 15, 16, 17, 18, 19, 20, 21, 23, 28

T
terrestrial 9
The global heat conveyor 27, 28
tides 18

U
Universe 3, 17